J959.1
H

BURMA (MYANMAR)

Nathaniel Harris

Marshall Cavendish
Benchmark
New York

This edition first published in 2010 in the United States of America by
MARSHALL CAVENDISH BENCHMARK
An imprint of Marshall Cavendish Corporation

Website: www.marshallcavendish.us

This publication represents the opinions and views of the author based on Nathaniel Harris's personal
experience, knowledge, and research. The information in this book serves as a general guide only. The author
and publisher have used their best efforts in preparing this book and disclaim liability rising directly and
indirectly from the use and application of this book.

Other Marshall Cavendish Offices:
Marshall Cavendish Ltd. 5th Floor, 32-38 Saffron Hill, London EC1N 8 FH, UK • Marshall Cavendish International
(Asia) Private Limited, 1 New Industrial Road, Singapore 536196 • Marshall Cavendish International (Thailand)
Co Ltd. 253 Asoke, 12th Flr, Sukhumvit 21 Road, Klongtoey Nua, Wattana, Bangkok 10110, Thailand • Marshall
Cavendish (Malaysia) Sdn Bhd, Times Subang, Lot 46, Subang Hi-Tech Industrial Park, Batu Tiga, 40000 Shah
Alam, Selangor Darul Ehsan, Malaysia

Marshall Cavendish is a trademark of Times Publishing Limited

All websites were available and accurate when this book was sent to press.

Library of Congress Cataloging-in-Publication Data

Harris, Nathaniel, 1937-
   Burma (Myanmar) / Nathaniel Harris.
      p. cm. — (Global hotspots)
   Includes index.
   Summary: "Discusses Burma, its history, conflicts, and the reasons why it is currently in the news"—Provided
by publisher.
   ISBN 978-0-7614-4758-0
   1. Burma—Juvenile literature. I. Title.
   DS527.4.H37 2011
959.1—dc22
                                    2009039785

First published in 2010 by
MACMILLAN EDUCATION AUSTRALIA PTY LTD
15–19 Claremont Street, South Yarra 3141

Visit our website at www.macmillan.com.au or go directly to www.macmillanlibrary.com.au

Associated companies and representatives throughout the world.

 Produced for Macmillan Education Australia by
MONKEY PUZZLE MEDIA LTD
48 York Avenue, Hove BN3 1PJ, UK

Edited by Susie Brooks
Text and cover design by Tom Morris and James Winrow
Page layout by Tom Morris
Photo research by Susie Brooks and Lynda Lines
Maps by Martin Darlison, Encompass Graphics

Printed in the United States

Acknowledgments
The author and the publisher are grateful to the following for permission to reproduce copyright material:

Front cover photograph: Monks sit in protest after Burmese riot police and military officials stopped their peaceful
march in Rangoon (Yangon) in 2007. Courtesy of Reuters (Adrees Latif).

Corbis, 6 (José Fuste Raga/zefa), 9 (Bettmann), 10 (Bettmann), 16 (Bettmann), 18 (Bettmann), 19 (Eric Preau/Sygma), 22
(Micheline Pelletier/Sygma), 28 (epa), 29 (Vivek Prakash/Reuters); Getty Images, 4 (AFP), 7 (De Agostini), 8 (Hulton Archive),
11 (Hulton Archive), 12 (Popperfoto), 14 (Time & Life Pictures), 15 (Hulton Archive), 20 (AFP), 21 (AFP), 23 (Time & Life
Pictures), 24 (AFP), 25 (Per-Anders Pettersson), 26 (AFP), 27 (AFP); iStockphoto, 30; Topfoto.co.uk 17 (RIA Novosti).

While every care has been taken to trace and acknowledge copyright, the publisher tenders their apologies for any
accidental infringement where copyright has proved untraceable. Where the attempt has been unsuccessful, the
publisher welcomes information that would redress the situation.

1 3 5 6 4 2

CONTENTS

ALWAYS IN THE NEWS 4

EARLY HISTORY 6

BURMA UNDER BRITISH RULE 8

CONQUERED BY JAPAN 10

INDEPENDENT BURMA 12

THE ARMED FORCES TAKE OVER 14

ONE-PARTY STATE 16

YEARS OF FAILURE 18

THE PEOPLE PROTEST 20

ELECTION TRIUMPH 22

BURMA UNDER THE ARMY 24

UPHEAVALS: 2003–2007 26

HOT SPOT BURMA 28

FIND OUT MORE 30

GLOSSARY 31

INDEX 32

Glossary Words

When a word is printed in **bold**, you can look up its meaning in the Glossary on page 31.

ALWAYS IN THE NEWS

Global hot spots are places that are always in the news. They are places where there has been conflict between different groups of people for years. Sometimes the conflicts have lasted for hundreds of years.

Why Do Hot Spots Happen?

There are four main reasons why hot spots happen:

1 Disputes over land, and who has the right to live on it.

2 Disagreements over religion and **culture**, where different peoples find it impossible to live happily side-by-side.

3 Arguments over how the government should be organized.

4 Conflict over resources, such as oil, gold, or diamonds.

Sometimes these disagreements spill over into violence—and into the headlines.

HOT SPOT BRIEFING

NAMES
In 1989, Burma's military government officially changed the country's name to Myanmar. But most people, and many foreign governments, continue to call it Burma to show their disapproval of military rule. Such people also prefer the old name of Burma's former capital city, Rangoon, to the government version, Yangon.

Burmese soldiers parade through the new capital city, Nay Pyi Taw, on Armed Forces Day, March 27, 2007. The army has dominated Burmese society since 1962.

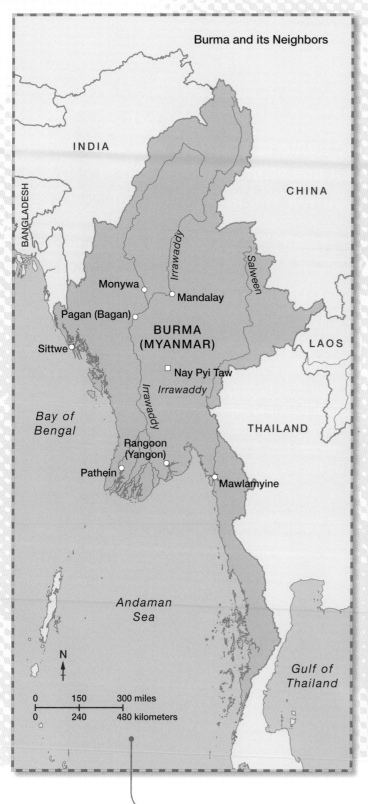

Burma and its Neighbors

INDIA

BANGLADESH

CHINA

Irrawaddy

Salween

Monywa

Mandalay

Pagan (Bagan)

BURMA
(MYANMAR)

LAOS

Sittwe

Nay Pyi Taw

Irrawaddy

Irrawaddy

Bay of
Bengal

THAILAND

Rangoon
(Yangon)

Pathein

Mawlamyine

Andaman
Sea

N

Gulf of
Thailand

| 0 | 150 | 300 miles |
| 0 | 240 | 480 kilometers |

Burma (Myanmar) shares borders with five other Asian countries. Since 2005, Nay Pyi Taw has replaced Rangoon (Yangon) as the Burmese capital city.

Burma and Army Rule

Burma has been a hot spot since 1962, when army leaders began to govern the country by force. The military rulers have made it very difficult for people to oppose them. Peaceful protesters have been shot down, and many **pro-democracy** leaders have been jailed or exiled. Even so, there are still Burmese people who are willing to challenge the military government.

Civil Wars

The Burmese army has fought long **civil wars** against the country's many **minority peoples**. The army's treatment of minorities has been particularly brutal.

A POOR PEOPLE

STATISTICS

Though the country is rich in resources, its people are poor.

- In terms of the wealth of its people, Burma is ranked 163rd of the 178 countries in the world.
- 32 percent of Burmese people live below the poverty line (the minimum needed to live reasonably).
- Many Burmese families survive on as little as $1.50 a day.

EARLY HISTORY

Early in its history, Burma became home to a variety of different peoples. At times it was a powerful kingdom. But in the 1800s, the British conquered Burma and made it part of their huge empire.

The Burmans Arrive

In the 800s CE, people called the Burmans moved into the country. For hundreds of years they fought with people in the south, called the Mons. It was not until the 1700s that the Burmans won control of most of Burma's central and southern lowlands.

HOT SPOT BRIEFING

BURMA'S FIRST CAPITAL
Pagan (or Bagan) in central Burma was the country's first capital (849–1284). Its kings were great builders. Even today there are an amazing 3,200 temples and monuments in the long-abandoned city.

Thousands of Buddhist temples rise from the landscape at Pagan, which is among the most famous and beautiful ancient sites in Southeast Asia.

Burma is Born

The Burmans gave their name to Burma. They had their own language and followed the **Buddhist** religion. They became the largest group in the country, though many other peoples settled there, especially in the highland areas. Burma is still a land of many peoples.

The Kingdom of Burma

Around 1000 CE, Burma became a kingdom. Some Burmese **dynasties** were very powerful. They united the country's people and waged war on neighboring Siam (modern Thailand). But between 1824 and 1885, the Burmese fought three disastrous wars against Britain. After the third war, Burma's king was **exiled** and the country became part of the British **Empire**.

HOT SPOT BRIEFING

KING ANIRUDDHA
Aniruddha was a warrior king who reigned from 1044 to 1077. He is still a great hero to the Burmese. His conquests made him the first ruler to control all of the land that is now Burma. He died after being gored by a wild bull.

British forces advance upriver during the first Anglo-Burmese war of 1824–1826. The Burmese resisted but had no chance against a disciplined modern army and its superior firepower.

BURMA UNDER BRITISH RULE

By 1885, the British had occupied all of Burma. However, they faced resistance from Burmese rebels, or **guerrillas**. It took five years of fighting and 30,000 British troops to bring Burma under full British control.

Far-reaching Changes

British rule brought far-reaching changes in Burma. The British drained swamps and built roads and railways. Burma became a great grower and exporter of rice, as well as producing timber and oil. Burmese students were able to study at the new Rangoon University and in Britain.

"The people seem young. They are never old. Life comes to them always as a pleasant thing... The people all seem happy."

A 1900s British view of the Burmese.

The first Burmese trains ran on the British-built Rangoon and Irrawaddy State Railway. The picture shows the opening ceremony, with a train getting up steam ready to depart, on June 23, 1877.

Burmese Discontent

Many Burmese were unhappy with British rule. British officials held all of the most important government positions. British companies dominated the Burmese economy. The Burmese also resented the large numbers of Indian workers and businessmen who came from British-ruled India and settled in Burma.

The Nationalist Movement

In the 1900s, a **nationalist** movement developed in Burma. Its members were determined to win independence from Britain. In 1937, the British granted Burma limited self-government, but many nationalists remained dissatisfied. Some hoped to end British rule by force. One group left Burma and began military training in Japan, a powerful nation that seemed friendly toward nationalist ideas.

HOT SPOT BRIEFING

BRITAIN'S ASIAN EMPIRE
Until the 1940s, Britain ruled a vast empire in Asia. The greatest British possession was India. British India consisted of present-day India, Pakistan, and Bangladesh. In addition, from 1885 to 1937, Burma was part of British India.

Mounted British police patrol a crowded Burmese street. The photograph dates from about 1930, when Burmese nationalists were beginning to challenge British rule.

CONQUERED BY JAPAN

In 1939, World War II broke out in Europe. In December 1941, Japan entered the war by attacking American ships in Pearl Harbor, Hawaii. Japan also attacked countries in Southeast Asia, including Burma.

Japan Victorious

The Japanese were victorious everywhere. In Burma they drove out British and **Commonwealth** forces, who retreated into India. A group of Japanese-trained Burmese nationalists, the "Thirty Comrades," returned to Burma with the Japanese. They formed the Burma Independence Army, fighting on the Japanese side.

"The Japanese from the first broke almost all the promises that they gave us."

Burmese leader, Aung San.

Japanese tanks cross a Burmese stream during their victorious advance in World War II.

A New Freedom?

The Japanese claimed to have come to free the Burmese and other Asian peoples from British control. In August 1943, Burma officially became independent. But in reality the Japanese continued to occupy Burma, and their rule was harsh.

The War Turns Against Japan

The war slowly turned against Japan in Asia and the Pacific. In November 1944, British and Indian forces advanced back into Burma. The Burmese nationalists, led by Aung San, one of the "Thirty Comrades," now changed sides and helped the British. The war ended in 1945 with Japan's surrender.

A British patrol lands at a Burmese riverside village, searching for Japanese soldiers. The British and their allies fought a bloody and immensely destructive war in Burma in 1945.

INDEPENDENT BURMA

The nationalist leader, Aung San, demanded independence for Burma from the British. The British agreed, and in 1947 elections were held to choose Burma's future government. Aung San's party won an overwhelming victory.

National Hero

Aung San's achievements have made him a Burmese national hero. However, he never lived to lead the country. In July 1947, he and some of his followers were shot dead by gunmen sent by a political rival.

HOT SPOT BRIEFING

AUNG SAN'S MURDER
The man behind Aung San's murder was a jealous rival, U Saw. U Saw had been a leading Burmese politician, but in the 1947 election his party was badly beaten. Following Aung San's murder, U Saw was put on trial, found guilty, and hanged.

In June 1947, Burmese leader Aung San marches at the head of a procession. He is the figure in white national dress, surrounded by Burmese soldiers. Less than a month later he was killed.

Independence

Burma finally became independent in January 1948. The government quickly declared the country a **republic**, and cut all ties with Britain and the Commonwealth. Burmese people were able to elect their own **parliament**. The first prime minister was a leading nationalist, U Nu.

Civil War

Not all Burmese supported U Nu's government. After independence, Burma was plunged into civil war. There were rebellions by parties who wanted political change, and by ex-soldiers and army units. Minority peoples such as the Rakhine, Kachin, and Karen also revolted, seeking independence from Burma. At times, Burma seemed about to fall apart.

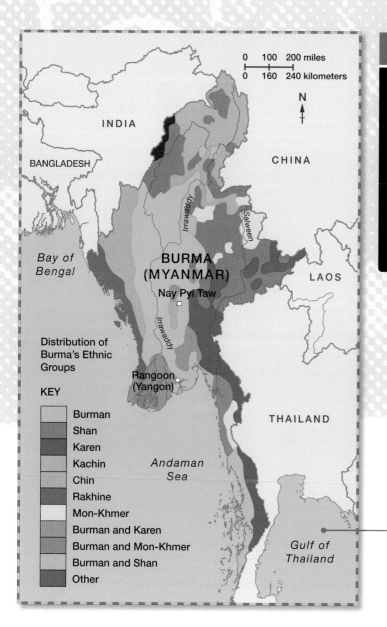

HOT SPOT BRIEFING

MINORITY PEOPLES
Minority peoples make up about a third of the Burmese population. Most live in the highlands close to the borders, or in coastal areas. Burma's peoples speak many different languages. They also follow different customs and sometimes different religions.

This map shows some of the main Burmese minority groups. There are actually more than 100 minority peoples in the country.

THE ARMED FORCES TAKE OVER

U Nu's government survived years of civil war. However, in 1958 there was a new crisis. U Nu's ruling political party split into rival groups, which made strong government impossible.

The Burmese prime minister, U Nu, takes part in public prayer. Nu was a devout Buddhist, and during his years in power he encouraged a religious revival.

Calling in the Army

U Nu was forced to ask the army to take over the government for a time. The army was widely respected. Years of fighting had turned it into a tough, professional force, led by an experienced general, Ne Win. The army restored order and carried out important **reforms**. In 1960, new elections were held and U Nu won a great victory.

HOT SPOT BRIEFING

TERMS OF RESPECT
In Burmese, "U" (as in U Nu) is a term of respect. It means roughly "Mr". "Daw" is the equivalent word for women.

The Army Turns Against U Nu

The army may have helped U Nu, but they also distrusted him. He was holding talks with minority peoples that the army had been fighting against for years. Army leaders felt that they were better at running Burma than the politicians. They began to plan a takeover of the government.

Tanks Enter Rangoon

On March 2, 1962, tanks rolled into Rangoon and the army took over after a **coup**. The army leader, Ne Win, became president of Burma. He was backed by a Revolutionary Council of military men. Together, they were determined to stay in power.

General Ne Win in October 1958, soon after becoming Burmese prime minister. At this time Ne Win had a great reputation as both soldier and politician.

ONE-PARTY STATE

Burma's new military rulers were determined to be obeyed. They imprisoned U Nu and other political leaders. People who opposed the army were severely punished, and newspapers and magazines were strictly controlled.

The Government's Plan

The military government published its plans for how the country would be run. The *Burmese Way to Socialism* declared that Burma was not to go back to **democracy**. Only one political party, the army-backed Burma Socialist Program Party, would be allowed.

HOT SPOT BRIEFING

THE INDIAN COMMUNITY
Many Indians settled in Burma while it was under British rule, and lived there for generations. But from 1964, the military government threw an estimated 400,000 Indians out of Burma.

In this 1967 photo, a man examines rice for sale in the black (illegal) market. Bad weather and government failures created shortages of once-abundant Burmese goods.

Government Control

The new leader, General Ne Win, wanted his government to control Burmese life completely. He **nationalized** industries, banks, and businesses and deliberately cut off Burma from the outside world. Foreigners became unwelcome, and Burmese people no longer studied or worked in other countries. The army stepped up its fight against minority peoples, who were still rebelling.

Rapid Change

The government carried out its plans rapidly, without much preparation. This had disastrous results. Production of goods and food fell. People lost their jobs, and goods were in such short supply that some had to be officially rationed, or shared out in limited amounts.

Ne Win is greeted by children in 1965, during a visit to Tashkent in Uzbekistan, Central Asia.

YEARS OF FAILURE

Burma's military rulers clung to power through many years of failure. In 1974, a **civilian** government replaced the Revolutionary Council, but Ne Win remained president. The other leaders were mainly ex-army men. Nothing really changed.

Signs of Discontent

Army rule was harsh, but some people dared to protest. In 1974, students seized the coffin of a popular and famous Burmese, U Thant, who had just died. This became the start of major anti-government demonstrations. Police and soldiers used their weapons to overpower the protesters.

HOT SPOT BRIEFING

U THANT
From 1961 to 1971, U Thant was Secretary-General of the **United Nations**. U Thant's peacemaking efforts made him the first internationally famous Burmese.

U Thant, Secretary-General of the United Nations, delivers a speech in 1970. The Burmese military leader, Ne Win, was hostile to Thant and probably jealous of his international reputation.

Savage Fighting

Fighting between the army and different rebel groups continued through the 1970s and became increasingly savage. Government soldiers uprooted entire villages to cut off the rebels' supplies. The army generally controlled the towns and lowlands, but it could not tame the guerrillas in the highland areas.

Improved Conditions

In the 1980s, Burma became more prosperous for a time. This was partly thanks to aid from foreign countries and the United Nations (UN). Nevertheless, in 1987 the UN described Burma as one of the world's least developed nations. This meant that it was behind most other countries in areas such as industry, living standards, health, and education.

A young fighter from the Karen ethnic group carries a rocket-propelled grenade. The Karen National Union has struggled for independence against the Burmese military government since 1949.

HOT SPOT BRIEFING

LUCKY NUMBER NINE
President Ne Win believed that the number 9 was lucky. In 1987, new Burmese money was issued. Notes of 10, 50 and 100 units were replaced by notes worth 9, 45 and 90 units—numbers that could be divided by lucky 9!

THE PEOPLE PROTEST

In 1988, Burmese anger with the government came to a head. A great movement in favor of democracy swept the country. However, the army used force to stay in power.

Growing Anger

People were angry because government actions had wiped out their savings and because there were food shortages. When students and ordinary people protested, some were killed by the army.

Ne Win Resigns

In July 1988, Ne Win resigned as head of the ruling party. He admitted that people no longer supported the government. He declared that there should be a vote to decide whether to return to democracy.

"If in future there are mob disturbances, if the army shoots, it hits—there is no firing in the air to scare."

Ne Win's resignation speech, July 23, 1988.

Demonstrators gathered in central Rangoon, as the anti-government protests of 1988 attracted more and more support.

Mass Demonstrations

From August 8, 1988, millions of Burmese marched the streets in favor of democracy. The army fired on the demonstrators but failed to stop them. When the soldiers withdrew, the pro-democracy movement seemed to have won.

The Army Strikes

On September 18, 1988, the army struck back against the democracy demonstrators. Hundreds of people were killed, and all opposition was crushed. Burma returned to military government under a new State Law and Order Council (SLORC for short).

Hundreds of thousands of Burmese surged through Rangoon on August 27, 1988, calling for democracy. There were similar scenes all over the country, until the army crushed the movement.

HOT SPOT BRIEFING

CHOSEN MOMENT
Many Burmese believe that some times and dates are lucky or favorable. The uprising of August 1988 was timed to start on "8-8-88" (August 8, 1988), at eight minutes past eight in the morning!

ELECTION TRIUMPH

The new military council, SLORC, suddenly changed many government policies. In 1989, it also changed the name of the country to Myanmar. Other places were renamed too, including the capital, Rangoon, which became Yangon.

New Policies

The SLORC promised **multi-party** elections and abandoned the *Burmese Way to Socialism*. People were encouraged to start businesses and trade for themselves.

New Political Parties

New political parties quickly appeared. Among them was the National League for Democracy (NLD), which opposed the SLORC. A woman, Aung San Suu Kyi, became the best known of its leaders. The government made things as difficult as possible for the NLD, and placed Aung San Suu Kyi under **house arrest**.

HOT SPOT BRIEFING

AUNG SAN SUU KYI
Aung San Suu Kyi is the daughter of the great Burmese hero, Aung San. She is an inspiring speaker and writer, and has spent long periods under arrest. Her plight has alerted the world to the struggle for democracy in Burma. In 1991, she was awarded the Nobel Peace Prize.

Aung San Suu Kyi lived outside Burma for years and married a British scholar. But after returning in 1988, she soon became a famous campaigner for democracy.

The General Election

In May 1990, the Burmese held their first general election in thirty years. The NLD won an overwhelming victory, gaining 392 of the 492 seats. In a democracy, leaders of the NLD would then have formed a government. But this country was not a democracy.

Hopes Dashed

The NLD's hopes of becoming the Burmese government were soon dashed. SLORC ignored the election result. It held on to power, declaring that it would have to prepare a new **constitution** before any political change could take place.

"We will prevail [win] because our cause is right, because our cause is just... History is on our side. Time is on our side."

Aung San Suu Kyi.

On election day, May 27, 1990, young supporters stand in front of portraits of National League for Democracy leaders. Aung San Suu Kyi, under house arrest since July 1989, is pictured on the right.

BURMA UNDER THE ARMY

All through the 1990s, the military government continued to rule by force. At times, though, it tried to gain more popular support by reaching an agreement with its opponent, the NLD.

The National Convention

In 1993, the government appointed a National Convention to create a Burmese constitution. The NLD took part at first, but soon walked out. After this, Aung San Suu Kyi was often placed under arrest. At times she was freed and held talks with the government. But no agreement was ever reached.

HOT SPOT BRIEFING

A NEW NAME
In 1997, the ruling State Law and Order Council was renamed the State Peace and Development Council. The government's new title was chosen so that it would sound less stern.

Aung San Suu Kyi speaks to the press in 1995, after talks with the government broke down. Aung San and her followers steadily refused to accept anything less than full democracy.

The Army's Strength

During the 1990s, the Burmese army became one of the largest in the world, with about 400,000 soldiers. Many rebel groups were forced to back down or agree to stop fighting with the army. Some rebels remained strong by selling illegal drugs and using the money to buy supplies and weapons.

Human Rights Abuses

Human rights abuses were still common in Burma. Government opponents were tortured and jailed. People were forced into working on public projects. Many children were taken from their families and used as soldiers.

This 1996 photograph shows young boys working on a building site in Rangoon (Yangon). Many Burmese children have to earn their own living or even serve in the army.

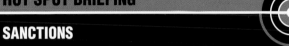

HOT SPOT BRIEFING

SANCTIONS
Many countries disapproved of the undemocratic Burmese government. From 1997, Australia, the **European Union**, the United States of America and other countries put legal limits, called **sanctions**, on their trade with Burma.

UPHEAVALS: 2003-2007

In 2003, a new prime minister, Khin Nyunt, proposed a "roadmap to democracy" for Burma. His ideas favored the military, but people still hoped that change might be on its way.

Army Power Struggle

In 2004, there was a power struggle within the army. Khin Nyunt lost and was removed as prime minister. The dominant military leader, General Than Shwe, took power. He seemed to be less friendly toward reforms, and people's hopes of democracy were weakened once more.

HOT SPOT BRIEFING

THE TSUNAMI
In December 2004, a **tsunami** devastated countries all around the Indian Ocean. Along the Burmese coast, twenty-nine villages were destroyed. The Burmese government did not ask for international help, but it did accept some aid.

Visiting India in 2004, Burmese army chief Than Shwe inspects a guard of honor. The Burmese military regime has several powerful Asian allies.

Still a Poor Country

In the 2000s, Burma remained a poor country. The army ran everything and the economy suffered because of sanctions on trade. New discoveries of oil and natural gas provided the government with money, and there was some **modernization**. But most Burmese civilians did not benefit.

Mass Demonstrations

In 2007, protests against low living standards set off the first mass demonstrations since 1988. In Rangoon, Buddhist **monks** took part in peaceful protests. The monks, in their saffron-colored robes, were normally treated with great respect. But the army moved in and crushed the "saffron revolution."

HOT SPOT BRIEFING

THE NEW CAPITAL
In 2005, the government announced that a new capital city, Nay Pyi Taw, had replaced the former capital, Rangoon (Yangon). When the first official ceremony took place in 2006, the new capital was a huge inland site, only partly built. The people who lived there were mainly government officials.

In September 2007, Buddhist monks marched in peaceful protest against the military government, only to be met with a violent response.

HOT SPOT BURMA

In 2008, the Burmese government finally recognized that it would never reach an agreement with the opposition. It published its own plan for a new constitution, and for a **referendum** on the plan.

The New Constitution

Under the new constitution, Burmese civilians would elect a parliament. However, the army would occupy a guaranteed quarter of all seats. In May 2008, the referendum was held, even though a devastating **cyclone** had hit the country only days earlier. The opposition refused to take part in the referendum. The government claimed that 92 percent of voters approved of the constitution.

CYCLONE NARGIS

STATISTICS

- In May 2008, Cyclone Nargis killed 78,000 people and left 56,000 missing, almost certainly dead.
- The UN estimated that 2.4 million survivors were close to starvation, and that 65 percent of the vital rice harvest was spoiled.

Burmese victims of the 2008 cyclone look sorrowfully at the wreckage of their village. The government was suspicious of outsiders, but eventually allowed foreign aid workers to help.

Still in Control

Decades after taking power, the Burmese military was still in control following the referendum. The army was bigger and stronger than ever. Aung San Suu Kyi and many other government opponents remained prisoners.

Army Failure

In most ways, army rule has failed the Burmese people. The country suffers from many problems, which military violence and domination have not solved. Human rights abuses continue to cause concern, and relations with other countries remain difficult. Burma seems likely to remain a hot spot for a long time to come.

Pro-democracy protests continue. In February 2009, these people arrived by bicycle at Hua Hin, Thailand, to demonstrate outside a meeting of Burmese and other Southeast Asian leaders.

FACTFINDER: Burma

Full name Union of Burma/Union of Myanmar

Capital Nay Pyi Taw

Area 261,970 square miles
(678,500 square kilometers)

Population 48,137,741 (July 2009 estimate)

Rate of population change +0.78% per year

Ethnic groups	Burman 68%
	Shan 9%
	Karen 7%
	Rakhine 4%
	Chinese 3%
	Indian 2%
	Mon 2%
	Other 5%

Industries Agricultural processing, wood and wood products, metals, cement

Gross Domestic Product* per person US$1,200

Percentage of labor force in agriculture 70%

Percentage of labor force in industry 7%

Percentage of labor force in services 23%

Number of phone lines 503,900

Number of TV stations 4 (in 2008)

Uncounted people The last official Burmese census (count of people) was in 1983. The last fully reliable count was in 1931. So all population figures are only estimates.

> * Gross Domestic Product, or GDP, is the value of all the goods and services produced by a country in a year. (Source for statistics: *CIA World Factbook*)

FOCUS QUESTIONS

These questions might help you to think about some of the issues raised in *Burma (Myanmar)*.

Leadership and Government

How have Burma's army leaders been able to stay in power for so long?

Economy

How has army control affected Burma's economy?
How much trade is Burma able to do with other countries?
Are foreign goods available in Burma?
Is Burma able to support itself in times of trouble?

Politics

Are Burma's relationships with other countries friendly?

Citizenship

Do you think the majority of people in Burma support army control?
Have Burmese people tried to challenge the army's control in any way?
What were the results?

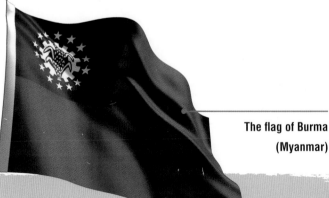

**The flag of Burma
(Myanmar)**

GLOSSARY

Buddhist follower of Buddhism, a religion based on the teachings of Buddha

civil war war between different groups within their own country

civilian non-military (civilians are people who are not soldiers)

Commonwealth organization that brings together Britain and a number of nations that were once part of the British Empire

constitution set of rules stating how a country will be governed

coup the sudden seizing of power by force

culture things that make a group of people distinctive, such as their language, clothes, food, music, songs, and stories

cyclone very powerful type of storm also known as a hurricane

democracy political system that allows people to vote for their government

dynasty family line of kings and queens

empire large group of countries ruled by a single country

exiled forced to live outside one's own country

European Union group of European countries that work closely together

guerrilla hit-and-run fighter, often one who aims to overthrow a government

house arrest forbidden to leave one's house

human rights abuses interfering with basic rights, such as the right to free speech

minority people smaller group of people within a larger group or population

modernization bringing up to date by using the latest ideas and technology

monk man who devotes himself to religion, withdrawing from everyday life

multi-party featuring a number of political parties

nationalized taken over by the government

nationalist wanting power or independence for one's own country

parliament group of members or representatives of a political nation

pro-democracy in favor of democracy

referendum vote on a single issue

reforms social or political changes

republic political system without a royal head of state

sanctions restrictions or penalties, threatened or carried out as punishment

tsunami giant tidal wave

United Nations organization set up after World War II that aims to help countries end disputes without fighting

INDEX

A
aid, 19, 26, 28
Anglo-Burmese war, 7
Aniruddha, King, 7
Armed Forces Day, 4, 11
army (*see also* military rule)
   against minority peoples,
     17
   civil wars, 5
   coup, 14, 15
   dominates society, 4
   fights rebels, 19
   rule, 16, 18, 24, 25, 29
   turns on Japanese, 11
Asian allies, 26
Aung San, 11, 12, 22
Aung San Suu Kyi, 22, 23,
   24, 29

B
black market, 16
British conquest, 6, 7
British Empire, 6, 7, 9
British rule, 8–9, 10, 11, 12,
   13
Buddhist religion, 6, 7, 14
Burma Socialist Program
   Party, 16
Burmans, 6, 7

C
child soldiers, 25
civil war, 5, 13, 14
civilian government, 18
Commonwealth, 10, 13
constitution, 23, 24, 28
coup, 15
cyclone, 28

E
economy, 9, 27
elections, 12, 13, 14, 22, 23,
   29

F
food shortages, 16, 20

H
human rights abuses, 25, 29

I
independence, 9, 11, 12, 13
Indians, 9, 11, 16

J
Japan, 9, 10–11

K
Kachin people, 13
Karen people, 13, 19
Khin Nyunt, 26

M
mass demonstrations, 21, 27
military rule, 4, 24, 26, 29
   Burma's name change, 22
   crushes opposition, 5, 21
   one-party state, 16
minority peoples, 5, 13, 15,
   17
monks, 27
Mon people, 6

N
National League for
   Democracy (NLD), 22, 23,
   24
nationalists, 9, 12
Nay Pyi Taw, 4, 5, 27
Ne Win, 14, 15, 17, 18, 19, 20

P
Pagan (Bagan), 5, 6
pro-democracy leaders, 5
protesters, 5, 18, 20
protests, 20, 21, 27, 29

R
railways, 8
Rakhine people, 13
Rangoon, 4, 5, 15, 20, 21,
   25, 27
   becomes Yangon, 22
rationing, 17
rebellions, 13
rebels, 19, 25
referendum, 28, 29
reforms, 14
religions, 6, 7, 13, 14
republic, 13
Revolutionary Council, 15, 18
roadmap to democracy, 26

S
sanctions, 25, 27
Siam (Thailand), 7
soldiers, 4, 25
State Law and Order Council
   (SLORC), 21, 22, 23, 24

T
temples, 6
Thailand, 5, 7
Than Shwe, 26
"Thirty Comrades," 10, 11, 17
tsunami, 26

U
U Nu, 13, 14, 15, 16
U Saw, 12
U Thant, 18
United Nations (UN), 18, 19, 28
uprising, 21

W
World War, II 10, 11

Y
Yangon (Rangoon), 4, 5, 22, 27